Dotty for Diamonds

◆ ◇ ◆ ◇ ◆ ◇ ◆ ◇ ◆ ◇ ◆

Copyright © 2019
Dotty for Diamonds
All rights reserved.

NAME OF DESIGN:

CANVAS SIZE: _____
PICTURE SIZE: _____
SQUARE DRILL ☐   ROUND DRILL ○

I PURCHASED THIS KIT FROM:
(OR IT WAS GIFTED BY)
_____

PRICE: ☐

DATE STARTED: / / /
DATE OF COMPLETION: / / /

ADVANCED
INTERMEDIATE
BEGINNER

HOW MUCH I LOVED THIS PROJECT ♡
◇ ◇ ◇ ◇ ◇

AFTER THE COMPLETION OF THIS PIECE I:
KEPT IT FOR MYSELF ◇   SOLD IT ◇
GIFTED IT TO A LOVED ONE ◇   OTHER ◇
I GIFTED IT TO: _____
OR I SOLD IT FOR ☐ ON/AT _____
_____ ON THE / / /

NOTES & IDEAS FOR THE NEXT PROJECT:
_____
_____
_____
_____

stick picture here

Name of design:

Canvas size: _____
Picture size: _____
Square drill ☐   Round drill ○

I purchased this kit from: _____
(or it was gifted by)

_____
Price: ☐

Advanced
Intermediate
Beginner

Date started: / / /
Date of completion: / / /

How much I loved this project ♡
◇ ◇ ◇ ◇ ◇

After the completion of this piece I:
Kept it for myself ◇   Sold it ◇
Gifted it to a loved one ◇   Other ◇
I gifted it to: _____
Or I sold it for ☐ on/at _____
_____ on the / / /

Notes & ideas for the next project:
_____
_____
_____
_____

◇·◇·◇·◇·◇·◇·◇·◇·◇·◇·◇·◇

stick picture here

Name of design:

Canvas size: _____
Picture size: _____
Square drill ☐   Round drill ○

I purchased this kit from:
(or it was gifted by)
_____
Price: [ ]

Advanced
Intermediate
Beginner

Date started: / /
Date of completion: / /

How much I loved this project ♡
◇ ◇ ◇ ◇ ◇

After the completion of this piece I:
Kept it for myself ◇   Sold it ◇
Gifted it to a loved one ◇   Other ◇
I gifted it to: _____
Or I sold it for [ ] on/at _____
_____ on the / /

Notes & ideas for the next project:
_____
_____
_____
_____

stick picture here

Name of design:

Canvas size: _____
Picture size: _____
Square drill ☐ Round drill ○

I purchased this kit from:
(or it was gifted by)
_____

Price: [   ]

Date started: / /
Date of completion: / /

Advanced
Intermediate
Beginner

How much I loved this project ♡
◇ ◇ ◇ ◇ ◇

After the completion of this piece I:
Kept it for myself ◇   Sold it ◇
Gifted it to a loved one ◇   Other ◇

I gifted it to: _____
Or I sold it for [   ] on/at _____
_____ on the / /

Notes & ideas for the next project:
_____
_____
_____
_____

stick picture here

NAME OF DESIGN:

CANVAS SIZE: _____
PICTURE SIZE: _____
SQUARE DRILL ☐   ROUND DRILL ○

DATE STARTED: _ / _ / _
DATE OF COMPLETION: _ / _ / _

I PURCHASED THIS KIT FROM:
(OR IT WAS GIFTED BY)
_____

ADVANCED
INTERMEDIATE
BEGINNER

HOW MUCH I LOVED THIS PROJECT ♡
◇ ◇ ◇ ◇ ◇

PRICE: ☐

AFTER THE COMPLETION OF THIS PIECE I:
KEPT IT FOR MYSELF ◇   SOLD IT ◇
GIFTED IT TO A LOVED ONE ◇   OTHER ◇

I GIFTED IT TO: _____
OR I SOLD IT FOR ☐ ON/AT _____
_____ ON THE _ / _ / _

NOTES & IDEAS FOR THE NEXT PROJECT:
_____
_____
_____
_____

stick picture here

Name of design:

Canvas size: _____
Picture size: _____
Square drill ☐   Round drill ○

Date started: / /
Date of completion: / /

I purchased this kit from:
(or it was gifted by)

Advanced
Intermediate
Beginner

How much I loved this project ♡
◇ ◇ ◇ ◇ ◇

_____
Price: ☐

After the completion of this piece I:
Kept it for myself ◇   Sold it ◇
Gifted it to a loved one ◇   Other ◇
I gifted it to: _____
Or I sold it for ☐ on/at _____
_____ on the / /

Notes & ideas for the next project:
_____
_____
_____
_____

stick picture here

Name of design:

Canvas size: _____
Picture size: _____
Square drill ☐   Round drill ○

I purchased this kit from: _____
(or it was gifted by)

Price: ☐

- Advanced
- Intermediate
- Beginner

Date started: / /
Date of completion: / /

How much I loved this project ♡
◇ ◇ ◇ ◇ ◇

After the completion of this piece I:
Kept it for myself ◇   Sold it ◇
Gifted it to a loved one ◇   Other ◇

I gifted it to: _____
Or I sold it for ☐ on/at _____
_____ on the / /

Notes & ideas for the next project:
_____
_____
_____
_____

stick picture here

NAME OF DESIGN:

CANVAS SIZE: _____
PICTURE SIZE: _____
SQUARE DRILL ☐   ROUND DRILL ○

DATE STARTED: / / /
DATE OF COMPLETION: / / /

I PURCHASED THIS KIT FROM:
(OR IT WAS GIFTED BY)
_____
PRICE: [____]

- ADVANCED
- INTERMEDIATE
- BEGINNER

HOW MUCH I LOVED THIS PROJECT ♡
◇ ◇ ◇ ◇ ◇

AFTER THE COMPLETION OF THIS PIECE I:
KEPT IT FOR MYSELF ◇   SOLD IT ◇
GIFTED IT TO A LOVED ONE ◇   OTHER ◇

I GIFTED IT TO: _____
OR I SOLD IT FOR [____] ON/AT _____
_____ ON THE / / /

NOTES & IDEAS FOR THE NEXT PROJECT:
_____
_____
_____
_____

stick picture here

Name of design:

Canvas size: _____
Picture size: _____
Square drill ☐   Round drill ○

I purchased this kit from:
(or it was gifted by)
_____

Price: [   ]

Advanced
Intermediate
Beginner

Date started: / /
Date of completion: / /

How much I loved this project ♡
◇ ◇ ◇ ◇ ◇

After the completion of this piece I:
Kept it for myself ◇   Sold it ◇
Gifted it to a loved one ◇   Other ◇

I gifted it to: _____
Or I sold it for [   ] on/at _____
_____ on the / /

Notes & ideas for the next project:
_____
_____
_____
_____

stick picture here

Name of design:

Canvas size: _____
Picture size: _____
Square drill ☐   Round drill ○

Date started: _ / _ / _
Date of completion: _ / _ / _

I purchased this kit from:
(or it was gifted by)

Advanced
Intermediate
Beginner

How much I loved this project ♡
◇ ◇ ◇ ◇ ◇

_____
Price: [ ]

After the completion of this piece I:
Kept it for myself ◇   Sold it ◇
Gifted it to a loved one ◇   Other ◇

I gifted it to: _____
Or I sold it for [ ] on/at _____
_____ on the _ / _ / _

Notes & ideas for the next project:
_____
_____
_____
_____

stick picture here

Name of design:

Canvas size: _____
Picture size: _____
Square drill ☐   Round drill ○

I purchased this kit from:
(or it was gifted by)
_____
Price: ☐

Advanced
Intermediate
Beginner

Date started: / / /
Date of completion: / / /

How much I loved this project ♡
◇ ◇ ◇ ◇ ◇

After the completion of this piece I:
Kept it for myself ◇   Sold it ◇
Gifted it to a loved one ◇   Other ◇

I gifted it to: _____
Or I sold it for ☐ on/at _____
_____ on the / / /

Notes & ideas for the next project:
_____
_____
_____
_____

stick picture here

Name of design:

Canvas size: _____
Picture size: _____
Square drill ☐   Round drill ○

I purchased this kit from:
(or it was gifted by)
_____
Price: ☐

Date started: / / /
Date of completion: / / /

Advanced
Intermediate
Beginner

How much I loved this project ♡
◇ ◇ ◇ ◇ ◇

After the completion of this piece I:
Kept it for myself ◇   Sold it ◇
Gifted it to a loved one ◇   Other ◇

I gifted it to: _____
Or I sold it for [   ] on/at _____
_____ on the / / /

Notes & ideas for the next project:
_____
_____
_____
_____

stick picture here

Name of design:

Canvas size: _____
Picture size: _____
Square drill ☐   Round drill ○

I purchased this kit from:
(or it was gifted by)
_____

Price: ☐

Advanced
Intermediate
Beginner

Date started: / / /
Date of completion: / / /

How much I loved this project ♡
◇ ◇ ◇ ◇ ◇

After the completion of this piece I:
Kept it for myself ◇   Sold it ◇
Gifted it to a loved one ◇   Other ◇

I gifted it to: _____
Or I sold it for ☐ **on/at** _____
_____ **on the** / / /

Notes & ideas for the next project:
_____
_____
_____

stick picture here

Name of design:

Canvas size: _____
Picture size: _____
Square drill ☐   Round drill ○

I purchased this kit from:
(or it was gifted by)
_____

Price: [   ]

- Advanced
- Intermediate
- Beginner

Date started: / /
Date of completion: / /

How much I loved this project ♡
◇ ◇ ◇ ◇ ◇

After the completion of this piece I:
Kept it for myself ◇   Sold it ◇
Gifted it to a loved one ◇   Other ◇

I gifted it to: _____
Or I sold it for [   ] on/at _____
_____ on the / /

Notes & ideas for the next project:
_____
_____
_____
_____

stick picture here

◇◇◇◇◇◇◇◇◇◇◇◇◇◇

Name of Design:

Canvas size: _____
Picture size: _____
Square drill ☐   Round drill ○

I purchased this kit from:
(or it was gifted by)
_____

Price: [ ]

Advanced
Intermediate
Beginner

Date started: / /
Date of completion: / /

How much I loved this project ♡
◇ ◇ ◇ ◇ ◇

After the completion of this piece I:
Kept it for myself ◇   Sold it ◇
Gifted it to a loved one ◇   Other ◇

I gifted it to: _____
Or I sold it for [ ] on/at _____
_____ on the / /

Notes & ideas for the next project:
_____
_____
_____
_____

stick picture here

Name of design:

Canvas size: _____
Picture size: _____
Square drill ☐   Round drill ○

I purchased this kit from:
(or it was gifted by)
_____

Price: ☐

Advanced
Intermediate
Beginner

Date started: / / /
Date of completion: / / /

How much I loved this project ♡
◇ ◇ ◇ ◇ ◇

After the completion of this piece I:
Kept it for myself ◇   Sold it ◇
Gifted it to a loved one ◇   Other ◇

I gifted it to: _____
Or I sold it for ☐ on/at _____
_____ on the / / /

Notes & ideas for the next project:
_____
_____
_____
_____

stick picture here

Name of design:

Canvas size: _____
Picture size: _____
Square drill ☐   Round drill ○

I purchased this kit from:
(or it was gifted by)
_____

Price: ☐

Date started: / / /
Date of completion: / / /

Advanced
Intermediate
Beginner

How much I loved this project ♡
◇ ◇ ◇ ◇ ◇

After the completion of this piece I:
Kept it for myself ◇   Sold it ◇
Gifted it to a loved one ◇   Other ◇

I gifted it to: _____
Or I sold it for ☐ on/at _____
_____ on the / / /

Notes & ideas for the next project:
_____
_____
_____
_____

◇◦◇◦◇◦◇◦◇◦◇◦◇◦◇◦◇◦◇◦◇◦◇◦◇

stick picture here

Name of design:

Canvas size: _____
Picture size: _____
Square drill ☐   Round drill ○

I purchased this kit from:
(or it was gifted by)
_____

Price: [____]

Date started: / /
Date of completion: / /

Advanced
Intermediate
Beginner

How much I loved this project ♡
◇ ◇ ◇ ◇ ◇

After the completion of this piece I:
Kept it for myself ◇   Sold it ◇
Gifted it to a loved one ◇   Other ◇

I gifted it to: _____
Or I sold it for [____] on/at _____
_____ on the / /

Notes & ideas for the next project:
_____
_____
_____
_____

stick picture here

Name of Design:

Canvas size: _____
Picture size: _____
Square drill ☐   Round drill ○

I purchased this kit from:
(or it was gifted by)
_____

Price: [ ]

Advanced / Intermediate / Beginner

Date started: / / /
Date of completion: / / /

How much I loved this project ♡
◇ ◇ ◇ ◇ ◇

After the completion of this piece I:
Kept it for myself ◇   Sold it ◇
Gifted it to a loved one ◇   Other ◇

I gifted it to: _____
Or I sold it for [ ] on/at _____
_____ on the / / /

Notes & ideas for the next project:
_____
_____
_____
_____

◇◇◇◇◇◇◇◇◇◇◇◇◇◇◇◇

stick picture here

Name of design:

Canvas size: _____
Picture size: _____
Square drill ☐   Round drill ○

Date started: _ / _ / _
Date of completion: _ / _ / _

I purchased this kit from:
(or it was gifted by)
_____

Price: ☐

- Advanced
- Intermediate
- Beginner

How much I loved this project ♡
◇ ◇ ◇ ◇ ◇

After the completion of this piece I:
Kept it for myself ◇   Sold it ◇
Gifted it to a loved one ◇   Other ◇

I gifted it to: _____
Or I sold it for [ ] on/at _____
_____ on the _ / _ / _

Notes & ideas for the next project:
_____
_____
_____

stick picture here

Name of design:

Canvas size: _____

Picture size: _____

Square drill ☐   Round drill ○

I purchased this kit from:
(or it was gifted by)
_____

Price: [____]

After the completion of this piece I:

Kept it for myself ◇   Sold it ◇

Gifted it to a loved one ◇   Other ◇

I gifted it to: _____

Or I sold it for [____] on/at _____

On the / /

Notes & ideas for the next project:

_____
_____
_____
_____

Date started: / / /

Date of completion: / / /

Advanced
Intermediate
Beginner

How much I loved this project ♡

◇ ◇ ◇ ◇ ◇

stick picture here

NAME OF DESIGN:

CANVAS SIZE: _____
PICTURE SIZE: _____
SQUARE DRILL ☐   ROUND DRILL ○

DATE STARTED: / / /
DATE OF COMPLETION: / / /

I PURCHASED THIS KIT FROM:
(OR IT WAS GIFTED BY)
_____
PRICE: ☐

ADVANCED
INTERMEDIATE
BEGINNER

HOW MUCH I LOVED THIS PROJECT ♡
◇ ◇ ◇ ◇ ◇

AFTER THE COMPLETION OF THIS PIECE I:
KEPT IT FOR MYSELF ◇   SOLD IT ◇
GIFTED IT TO A LOVED ONE ◇   OTHER ◇

I GIFTED IT TO: _____
OR I SOLD IT FOR ☐ ON/AT _____
_____ ON THE / / /

NOTES & IDEAS FOR THE NEXT PROJECT:
_____
_____
_____
_____

stick picture here

Name of design:

Canvas size: _____
Picture size: _____
Square drill ☐   Round drill ○

I purchased this kit from:
(or it was gifted by)
_____

Price: [ ]

- Advanced
- Intermediate
- Beginner

Date started: / / /
Date of completion: / / /

How much I loved this project ♡
◇ ◇ ◇ ◇ ◇

After the completion of this piece I:
Kept it for myself ◇   Sold it ◇
Gifted it to a loved one ◇   Other ◇

I gifted it to: _____
Or I sold it for [ ] on/at _____
_____ on the / / /

Notes & ideas for the next project:
_____
_____
_____
_____

stick picture here

Name of design:

Canvas size: _____
Picture size: _____
Square drill ☐   Round drill ○

I purchased this kit from:
(or it was gifted by)
_____
Price: ☐

- Advanced
- Intermediate
- Beginner

Date started: / /
Date of completion: / /

How much I loved this project ♡
◇ ◇ ◇ ◇ ◇

After the completion of this piece I:
Kept it for myself ◇   Sold it ◇
Gifted it to a loved one ◇   Other ◇

I gifted it to: _____
Or I sold it for ☐ on/at _____
_____ on the / /

Notes & ideas for the next project:
_____
_____
_____
_____

stick picture here

Name of design:

Canvas size: _____
Picture size: _____
Square drill ☐   Round drill ○

Date started: _/_/_
Date of completion: _/_/_

I purchased this kit from:
(or it was gifted by)
_____

- Advanced
- Intermediate
- Beginner

How much I loved this project ♡
◇ ◇ ◇ ◇ ◇

Price: ☐

After the completion of this piece I:
Kept it for myself ◇   Sold it ◇
Gifted it to a loved one ◇   Other ◇

I gifted it to: _____
Or I sold it for ☐ on/at _____
_____ on the _/_/_

Notes & ideas for the next project:
_____
_____
_____
_____

◇◇◇◇◇◇◇◇◇◇◇◇◇◇

stick picture here

Name of design:

Canvas size: _____
Picture size: _____
Square drill ☐   Round drill ○

I purchased this kit from:
(or it was gifted by)
_____

Price: ☐

Advanced
Intermediate
Beginner

Date started: / / /
Date of completion: / / /

How much I loved this project ♡
◇ ◇ ◇ ◇ ◇

After the completion of this piece I:
Kept it for myself ◇   Sold it ◇
Gifted it to a loved one ◇   Other ◇

I gifted it to: _____
Or I sold it for ☐ on/at _____
_____ on the / / /

Notes & ideas for the next project:
_____
_____
_____
_____

stick picture here

Name of design:

Canvas size: _____
Picture size: _____
Square drill ☐   Round drill ○

Date started: / /
Date of completion: / /

I purchased this kit from: _____
(or it was gifted by)

- Advanced
- Intermediate
- Beginner

How much I loved this project ♡
◇ ◇ ◇ ◇ ◇

Price: [ ]

After the completion of this piece I:
Kept it for myself ◇   Sold it ◇
Gifted it to a loved one ◇   Other ◇

I gifted it to: _____
Or I sold it for [ ] on/at _____
_____ on the / /

Notes & ideas for the next project:
_____
_____
_____
_____

stick picture here

Name of design:

Canvas size: _____
Picture size: _____
Square drill ☐   Round drill ○

Date started: _ / _ / _
Date of completion: _ / _ / _

I purchased this kit from: _____
(or it was gifted by)

Advanced
Intermediate
Beginner

How much I loved this project ♡
◇ ◇ ◇ ◇ ◇

Price: ☐

After the completion of this piece I:
Kept it for myself ◇   Sold it ◇
Gifted it to a loved one ◇   Other ◇

I gifted it to: _____
Or I sold it for ☐ on/at _____
_____ on the _ / _ / _

Notes & ideas for the next project:
_____
_____
_____
_____

◇·◇·◇·◇·◇·◇·◇·◇·◇·◇·◇·◇·◇·◇

stick picture here

Name of design:

Canvas size: _____
Picture size: _____
Square drill ☐   Round drill ○

Date started: / / /
Date of completion: / / /

I purchased this kit from:
(or it was gifted by)
_____

Advanced
Intermediate
Beginner

How much I loved this project ♡
◇ ◇ ◇ ◇ ◇

Price: ☐

After the completion of this piece I:

Kept it for myself ◇   Sold it ◇
Gifted it to a loved one ◇   Other ◇

I gifted it to: _____
Or I sold it for ☐ on/at _____
_____ on the / / /

Notes & ideas for the next project:
_____
_____
_____
_____

◇◇◇◇◇◇◇◇◇◇◇◇◇◇◇◇◇◇

stick picture here

NAME OF DESIGN:

CANVAS SIZE: _____
PICTURE SIZE: _____
SQUARE DRILL ☐   ROUND DRILL ○

DATE STARTED: / /
DATE OF COMPLETION: / /

I PURCHASED THIS KIT FROM:
(OR IT WAS GIFTED BY)
_____
PRICE: [____]

- ADVANCED
- INTERMEDIATE
- BEGINNER

HOW MUCH I LOVED THIS PROJECT ♡
◇ ◇ ◇ ◇ ◇

AFTER THE COMPLETION OF THIS PIECE I:
KEPT IT FOR MYSELF ◇   SOLD IT ◇
GIFTED IT TO A LOVED ONE ◇   OTHER ◇

I GIFTED IT TO: _____
OR I SOLD IT FOR [____] ON/AT _____
_____ ON THE / /

NOTES & IDEAS FOR THE NEXT PROJECT:
_____
_____
_____
_____

stick picture here

Name of design:

Canvas size: _____
Picture size: _____
Square drill ☐   Round drill ○

I purchased this kit from:
(or it was gifted by)
_____
Price: [ ]

Advanced
Intermediate
Beginner

Date started: / / /
Date of completion: / / /

How much I loved this project ♡
◇ ◇ ◇ ◇ ◇

After the completion of this piece I:
Kept it for myself ◇   Sold it ◇
Gifted it to a loved one ◇   Other ◇

I gifted it to: _____
Or I sold it for [ ] on/at _____
_____ on the / / /

Notes & ideas for the next project:
_____
_____
_____
_____

stick picture here

Name of design:

Canvas size: _____
Picture size: _____
Square drill ☐   Round drill ○

Date started: _/_/_
Date of completion: _/_/_

I purchased this kit from:
(or it was gifted by)
_____

- Advanced
- Intermediate
- Beginner

How much I loved this project ♡
◇ ◇ ◇ ◇ ◇

Price: [_____]

After the completion of this piece I:
Kept it for myself ◇   Sold it ◇
Gifted it to a loved one ◇   Other ◇

I gifted it to: _____
Or I sold it for [_____] on/at _____
_____ on the _/_/_

Notes & ideas for the next project:
_____
_____
_____
_____

stick picture here

NAME OF DESIGN:

CANVAS SIZE: _____

PICTURE SIZE: _____

SQUARE DRILL ☐   ROUND DRILL ○

DATE STARTED: _ / _ / _

DATE OF COMPLETION: _ / _ / _

I PURCHASED THIS KIT FROM:
(OR IT WAS GIFTED BY)
_____

PRICE: [ ]

ADVANCED
INTERMEDIATE
BEGINNER

HOW MUCH I LOVED THIS PROJECT ♡
◇ ◇ ◇ ◇ ◇

AFTER THE COMPLETION OF THIS PIECE I:

KEPT IT FOR MYSELF ◇   SOLD IT ◇

GIFTED IT TO A LOVED ONE ◇   OTHER ◇

I GIFTED IT TO: _____

OR I SOLD IT FOR [ ] ON/AT _____

ON THE _ / _ / _

NOTES & IDEAS FOR THE NEXT PROJECT:

_____
_____
_____
_____

stick picture here

◇◇◇◇◇◇◇◇◇◇◇◇◇◇◇◇

Name of design:

Canvas size: _____
Picture size: _____
Square drill ☐   Round drill ○

Date started: _/_/_
Date of completion: _/_/_

I purchased this kit from:
(or it was gifted by)

- Advanced
- Intermediate
- Beginner

How much I loved this project ♡
◇ ◇ ◇ ◇ ◇

_____
Price: ☐

After the completion of this piece I:
Kept it for myself ◇   Sold it ◇
Gifted it to a loved one ◇   Other ◇

I gifted it to: _____
Or I sold it for ☐ on/at _____
_____ on the _/_/_

Notes & ideas for the next project:
_____
_____
_____
_____

stick picture here

Name of design:

Canvas size: _____
Picture size: _____
Square drill ☐   Round drill ○

I purchased this kit from:
(or it was gifted by)
_____
Price: [ ]

Date started: / / /
Date of completion: / / /

Advanced
Intermediate
Beginner

How much I loved this project ♡
◇ ◇ ◇ ◇ ◇

After the completion of this piece I:
Kept it for myself ◇   Sold it ◇
Gifted it to a loved one ◇   Other ◇

I gifted it to: _____
Or I sold it for [ ] on/at _____
_____ on the / / /

Notes & ideas for the next project:
_____
_____
_____
_____

stick picture here

Name of design:

Canvas size: _____

Picture size: _____

Square drill ☐   Round drill ○

I purchased this kit from:
(or it was gifted by)

_____

Price: ☐

Advanced
Intermediate
Beginner

Date started: / / /

Date of completion: / / /

How much I loved this project ♡

◇ ◇ ◇ ◇ ◇

After the completion of this piece I:

Kept it for myself ◇   Sold it ◇

Gifted it to a loved one ◇   Other ◇

I gifted it to: _____

Or I sold it for [   ] on/at _____

_____ on the / / /

Notes & ideas for the next project:

_____
_____
_____
_____

stick picture here

◇·◇·◇·◇·◇·◇·◇·◇·◇·◇·◇·◇

Name of design:

Canvas size: _____
Picture size: _____
Square drill ☐   Round drill ○

I purchased this kit from:
(or it was gifted by)
_____
Price: [ ]

Date started: / / /
Date of completion: / / /

Advanced
Intermediate
Beginner

How much I loved this project ♡
◇ ◇ ◇ ◇ ◇

After the completion of this piece I:
Kept it for myself ◇   Sold it ◇
Gifted it to a loved one ◇   Other ◇

I gifted it to: _____
Or I sold it for [ ] on/at _____
On the / / /

Notes & ideas for the next project:
_____
_____
_____
_____

stick picture here

Name of Design:

Canvas size: _____
Picture size: _____
Square drill ☐   Round drill ○

Date started: / /
Date of completion: / /

I purchased this kit from:
(or it was gifted by)
_____

Price: [   ]

Advanced
Intermediate
Beginner

How much I loved this project ♡
◇ ◇ ◇ ◇ ◇

After the completion of this piece I:
Kept it for myself ◇   Sold it ◇
Gifted it to a loved one ◇   Other ◇

I gifted it to: _____
Or I sold it for [   ] on/at _____
_____ on the / /

Notes & ideas for the next project:
_____
_____
_____
_____

◇·◇·◇·◇·◇·◇·◇·◇·◇·◇·◇·◇·◇

stick picture here

Name of Design:

Canvas size: _____
Picture size: _____
Square drill ☐   Round drill ○

I purchased this kit from: _____
(or it was gifted by)

Price: [____]

Advanced
Intermediate
Beginner

Date started: / /
Date of completion: / /

How much I loved this project ♡
◇ ◇ ◇ ◇ ◇

After the completion of this piece I:
Kept it for myself ◇   Sold it ◇
Gifted it to a loved one ◇   Other ◇

I gifted it to: _____
Or I sold it for [____] on/at _____
_____ on the / /

Notes & ideas for the next project:
_____
_____
_____
_____

stick picture here

Name of design:

Canvas size: _____
Picture size: _____
Square drill ☐   Round drill ○

I purchased this kit from:
(or it was gifted by)

_____
Price: ☐

Date started: / / /
Date of completion: / / /

Advanced
Intermediate
Beginner

How much I loved this project ♡
◇ ◇ ◇ ◇ ◇

After the completion of this piece I:
Kept it for myself ◇   Sold it ◇
Gifted it to a loved one ◇   Other ◇

I gifted it to: _____
Or I sold it for ☐ on/at _____
_____ on the / / /

Notes & ideas for the next project:
_____
_____
_____
_____

stick picture here

Name of design:

Canvas size: _____

Picture size: _____

Square drill ☐   Round drill ○

I purchased this kit from:
(or it was gifted by)

_____

Price: ☐

Date started: / / /

Date of completion: / / /

- Advanced
- Intermediate
- Beginner

How much I loved this project ♡

◇ ◇ ◇ ◇ ◇

After the completion of this piece I:

Kept it for myself ◇   Sold it ◇

Gifted it to a loved one ◇   Other ◇

I gifted it to: _____

Or I sold it for ☐ on/at _____

_____ on the / / /

Notes & ideas for the next project:

_____
_____
_____
_____

stick picture here

NAME OF DESIGN:

CANVAS SIZE: _____
PICTURE SIZE: _____
SQUARE DRILL ☐   ROUND DRILL ○

DATE STARTED: / / /
DATE OF COMPLETION: / / /

I PURCHASED THIS KIT FROM:
(OR IT WAS GIFTED BY)
_____

- ADVANCED
- INTERMEDIATE
- BEGINNER

HOW MUCH I LOVED THIS PROJECT ♡
◇ ◇ ◇ ◇ ◇

PRICE: [ ]

AFTER THE COMPLETION OF THIS PIECE I:
KEPT IT FOR MYSELF ◇   SOLD IT ◇
GIFTED IT TO A LOVED ONE ◇   OTHER ◇

I GIFTED IT TO: _____
OR I SOLD IT FOR [ ] ON/AT _____
_____ ON THE / / /

NOTES & IDEAS FOR THE NEXT PROJECT:
_____
_____
_____
_____

◇·◇·◇·◇·◇·◇·◇·◇·◇·◇·◇·◇·◇·◇·◇·◇

stick picture here

Name of design:

Canvas size: _____
Picture size: _____
Square drill ☐   Round drill ○

I purchased this kit from: _____
(or it was gifted by)

Price: [ ]

Date started: / / /
Date of completion: / / /

◇ Advanced
◇ Intermediate
◇ Beginner

How much I loved this project ♡
◇ ◇ ◇ ◇ ◇

After the completion of this piece I:

Kept it for myself ◇   Sold it ◇

Gifted it to a loved one ◇   Other ◇

I gifted it to: _____
Or I sold it for [ ] on/at _____
_____ on the / / /

Notes & ideas for the next project:

_____
_____
_____
_____

stick picture here

Name of design:

Canvas size: _____

Picture size: _____

Square drill ☐   **Round drill** ○

I purchased this kit from:
(or it was gifted by)
_____

Price: ☐

- Advanced
- Intermediate
- Beginner

Date started: / / /

Date of completion: / / /

How much I loved this project ♡
◇ ◇ ◇ ◇ ◇

After the completion of this piece I:

Kept it for myself ◇   Sold it ◇

Gifted it to a loved one ◇   Other ◇

I gifted it to: _____

Or I sold it for ☐ on/at _____

_____ on the / / /

Notes & ideas for the next project:

_____
_____
_____
_____

stick picture here

Name of design:

Canvas size: _____

Picture size: _____

Square drill ☐ **Round drill** ○

I purchased this kit from:
(or it was gifted by)
_____

Price: ☐

- Advanced
- Intermediate
- Beginner

Date started: / / /

Date of completion: / / /

How much I loved this project ♡
◇ ◇ ◇ ◇ ◇

After the completion of this piece I:

Kept it for myself ◇ Sold it ◇

Gifted it to a loved one ◇ Other ◇

I gifted it to: _____

Or I sold it for ☐ on/at _____

_____ on the / / /

Notes & ideas for the next project:

_____
_____
_____
_____

stick picture here

Name of design: _____

Canvas size: _____
Picture size: _____
Square drill ☐   **Round drill** ○

I purchased this kit from:
(or it was gifted by)
_____
Price: [ ]

- Advanced
- Intermediate
- Beginner

Date started: / /
Date of completion: / /

How much I loved this project ♡
◇ ◇ ◇ ◇ ◇

After the completion of this piece I:
Kept it for myself ◇   Sold it ◇
Gifted it to a loved one ◇   Other ◇

I gifted it to: _____
Or I sold it for [ ] **on/at** _____
_____ **on the** / /

Notes & ideas for the next project:
_____
_____
_____
_____

◇·◇·◇·◇·◇·◇·◇·◇·◇·◇·◇·◇·◇·◇◇·◇

stick picture here

Name of design:

Canvas size: _____
Picture size: _____
Square drill ☐   Round drill ○

I purchased this kit from:
(or it was gifted by)
_____
Price: ☐

Date started: / /
Date of completion: / /

- Advanced
- Intermediate
- Beginner

How much I loved this project ♡
◇ ◇ ◇ ◇ ◇

After the completion of this piece I:
Kept it for myself ◇   Sold it ◇
Gifted it to a loved one ◇   Other ◇

I gifted it to: _____
Or I sold it for [ ] on/at _____
_____ on the / /

Notes & ideas for the next project:
_____
_____
_____
_____

stick picture here

NAME OF DESIGN:

CANVAS SIZE: _____

PICTURE SIZE: _____

SQUARE DRILL ☐   ROUND DRILL ○

DATE STARTED: / / /

DATE OF COMPLETION: / / /

I PURCHASED THIS KIT FROM:
(OR IT WAS GIFTED BY)

- ADVANCED
- INTERMEDIATE
- BEGINNER

HOW MUCH I LOVED THIS PROJECT ♡

◇ ◇ ◇ ◇ ◇

_____

PRICE: ☐

AFTER THE COMPLETION OF THIS PIECE I:

KEPT IT FOR MYSELF ◇   SOLD IT ◇

GIFTED IT TO A LOVED ONE ◇   OTHER ◇

I GIFTED IT TO: _____

OR I SOLD IT FOR ☐ ON/AT _____

_____ ON THE / / /

NOTES & IDEAS FOR THE NEXT PROJECT:

_____
_____
_____
_____

◇·◇·◇·◇·◇·◇·◇·◇·◇·◇·◇·◇·◇·◇·◇

stick picture here

Name of design:

Canvas size: _____
Picture size: _____
Square drill ☐   Round drill ○

Date started: / / /
Date of completion: / / /

I purchased this kit from:
(or it was gifted by)
_____

Price: ☐

- Advanced
- Intermediate
- Beginner

How much I loved this project ♡
◇ ◇ ◇ ◇ ◇

After the completion of this piece I:

Kept it for myself ◇   Sold it ◇

Gifted it to a loved one ◇   Other ◇

I gifted it to: _____
Or I sold it for ☐ on/at _____
_____ on the / / /

Notes & ideas for the next project:
_____
_____
_____
_____

stick picture here

Name of Design:

Canvas size: _____
Picture size: _____
Square drill ☐   Round drill ○

I purchased this kit from:
(or it was gifted by)
_____
Price: [ ]

- Advanced
- Intermediate
- Beginner

Date started: / / /
Date of completion: / / /

How much I loved this project ♡
◇ ◇ ◇ ◇ ◇

After the completion of this piece I:
Kept it for myself ◇   Sold it ◇
Gifted it to a loved one ◇   Other ◇

I gifted it to: _____
Or I sold it for [ ] on/at _____
_____ on the / / /

Notes & ideas for the next project:
_____
_____
_____
_____

◇·◇·◇·◇·◇·◇·◇·◇·◇·◇·◇·◇·◇·◇

stick picture here

NAME OF DESIGN:

CANVAS SIZE: _____

PICTURE SIZE: _____

SQUARE DRILL ☐ **ROUND DRILL** ○

I PURCHASED THIS KIT FROM:
(OR IT WAS GIFTED BY)
_____

PRICE: ☐

DATE STARTED: / /

DATE OF COMPLETION: / /

- ADVANCED
- INTERMEDIATE
- BEGINNER

HOW MUCH I LOVED THIS PROJECT ♡

◇ ◇ ◇ ◇ ◇

AFTER THE COMPLETION OF THIS PIECE I:

KEPT IT FOR MYSELF ◇   SOLD IT ◇

GIFTED IT TO A LOVED ONE ◇   OTHER ◇

I GIFTED IT TO: _____

OR I SOLD IT FOR ☐ ON/AT _____

_____ ON THE / /

NOTES & IDEAS FOR THE NEXT PROJECT:

_____
_____
_____
_____

stick picture here

Name of design:

Canvas size: _____
Picture size: _____
Square drill ☐   Round drill ○

I purchased this kit from:
(or it was gifted by)
_____
Price: [____]

Advanced
Intermediate
Beginner

Date started: __/__/__
Date of completion: __/__/__

How much I loved this project ♥
◇ ◇ ◇ ◇ ◇

After the completion of this piece I:
Kept it for myself ◇   Sold it ◇
Gifted it to a loved one ◇   Other ◇

I gifted it to: _____
Or I sold it for [____] on/at _____
_____ on the __/__/__

Notes & ideas for the next project:
_____
_____
_____
_____

stick picture here

Name of design:

Canvas size: _____

Picture size: _____

Square drill ☐   Round drill ○

I purchased this kit from: _____
(or it was gifted by)

Price: [ ]

- Advanced
- Intermediate
- Beginner

Date started: _/_/_

Date of completion: _/_/_

How much I loved this project ♡

◇ ◇ ◇ ◇ ◇

After the completion of this piece I:

Kept it for myself ◇   Sold it ◇

Gifted it to a loved one ◇   Other ◇

I gifted it to: _____

Or I sold it for [ ] on/at _____

_____ on the _/_/_

Notes & ideas for the next project:

_____
_____
_____
_____

◇◇◇◇◇◇◇◇◇◇◇◇◇◇◇◇

stick picture here

Name of Design:

Canvas size: _____
Picture size: _____
Square drill ☐   Round drill ○

I purchased this kit from:
(or it was gifted by)
_____

Price: [____]

Date started: / /
Date of completion: / /

Advanced
Intermediate
Beginner

How much I loved this project ♡
◇ ◇ ◇ ◇ ◇

After the completion of this piece I:
Kept it for myself ◇   Sold it ◇
Gifted it to a loved one ◇   Other ◇

I gifted it to: _____
Or I sold it for [____] on/at _____
_____ on the / /

Notes & ideas for the next project:
_____
_____
_____
_____

stick picture here

Name of design:

Canvas size: _____
Picture size: _____
Square drill ☐   Round drill ○

I purchased this kit from:
(or it was gifted by)
_____

Price: _____

Advanced
Intermediate
Beginner

Date started: / / /
Date of completion: / / /

How much I loved this project ♡
◇ ◇ ◇ ◇ ◇

After the completion of this piece I:
Kept it for myself ◇   Sold it ◇
Gifted it to a loved one ◇   Other ◇

I gifted it to: _____
Or I sold it for [____] on/at _____
_____ on the / / /

Notes & ideas for the next project:
_____
_____
_____
_____

stick picture here

NAME OF DESIGN:

CANVAS SIZE: _____
PICTURE SIZE: _____
SQUARE DRILL ☐   ROUND DRILL ○

I PURCHASED THIS KIT FROM:
(OR IT WAS GIFTED BY)
_____

PRICE: ☐

DATE STARTED: / / /
DATE OF COMPLETION: / / /

◇ ADVANCED
◇ INTERMEDIATE
◇ BEGINNER

HOW MUCH I LOVED THIS PROJECT ♡
◇ ◇ ◇ ◇ ◇

AFTER THE COMPLETION OF THIS PIECE I:
KEPT IT FOR MYSELF ◇   SOLD IT ◇
GIFTED IT TO A LOVED ONE ◇   OTHER ◇

I GIFTED IT TO: _____
OR I SOLD IT FOR ☐ ON/AT _____
_____ ON THE / / /

NOTES & IDEAS FOR THE NEXT PROJECT:
_____
_____
_____
_____

stick picture here

◇○◇○◇○◇○◇○◇○◇○◇○◇○◇○◇

Name of design:

Canvas size: _____
Picture size: _____
Square drill ☐   Round drill ○

I purchased this kit from:
(or it was gifted by)
_____

Price: [____]

Advanced
Intermediate
Beginner

Date started: __ / __ / __
Date of completion: __ / __ / __

How much I loved this project ♡
◇ ◇ ◇ ◇ ◇

After the completion of this piece I:
Kept it for myself ◇   Sold it ◇
Gifted it to a loved one ◇   Other ◇

I gifted it to: _____
Or I sold it for [____] on/at _____
_____ on the __ / __ / __

Notes & ideas for the next project:
_____
_____
_____
_____

stick picture here

Name of Design:

Canvas size: _____
Picture size: _____
Square drill ☐   Round drill ○

I purchased this kit from:
(or it was gifted by)
_____
Price: ☐

Date started: / /
Date of completion: / /

Advanced
Intermediate
Beginner

How much I loved this project ♡
◇ ◇ ◇ ◇ ◇

After the completion of this piece I:
Kept it for myself ◇   Sold it ◇
Gifted it to a loved one ◇   Other ◇

I gifted it to: _____
Or I sold it for ☐ on/at _____
_____ on the / /

Notes & ideas for the next project:
_____
_____
_____
_____

◇·◇·◇·◇·◇·◇·◇·◇·◇·◇·◇·◇·◇·◇

stick picture here

NAME OF DESIGN:

CANVAS SIZE: _____
PICTURE SIZE: _____
SQUARE DRILL ☐   ROUND DRILL ○

DATE STARTED: / /
DATE OF COMPLETION: / /

I PURCHASED THIS KIT FROM:
(OR IT WAS GIFTED BY)
_____

ADVANCED
INTERMEDIATE
BEGINNER

HOW MUCH I LOVED THIS PROJECT ♡
◇ ◇ ◇ ◇ ◇

PRICE: ☐

AFTER THE COMPLETION OF THIS PIECE I:

KEPT IT FOR MYSELF ◇   SOLD IT ◇

GIFTED IT TO A LOVED ONE ◇   OTHER ◇

I GIFTED IT TO: _____
OR I SOLD IT FOR ☐ ON/AT _____
_____ ON THE / /

NOTES & IDEAS FOR THE NEXT PROJECT:
_____
_____
_____
_____

◇◇◇◇◇◇◇◇◇◇◇◇◇◇◇◇◇

stick picture here

Name of design:

Canvas size: _____
Picture size: _____
Square drill ▢   Round drill ○

I purchased this kit from:
(or it was gifted by)
_____

Price: [____]

Date started: / /
Date of completion: / /

- Advanced
- Intermediate
- Beginner

How much I loved this project ♡
◇ ◇ ◇ ◇ ◇

After the completion of this piece I:

Kept it for myself ◇   Sold it ◇
Gifted it to a loved one ◇   Other ◇

I gifted it to: _____
Or I sold it for [____] on/at _____
_____ on the / /

Notes & ideas for the next project:
_____
_____
_____
_____

stick picture here

Name of design:

Canvas size: _____
Picture size: _____
Square drill ☐   Round drill ○

I purchased this kit from:
(or it was gifted by)
_____

Price: [ ]

After the completion of this piece I:
Kept it for myself ◇   Sold it ◇
Gifted it to a loved one ◇   Other ◇

I gifted it to: _____
Or I sold it for [ ] on/at _____
_____ on the / /

Notes & ideas for the next project:
_____
_____
_____
_____

Date started: / / /
Date of completion: / / /

- Advanced
- Intermediate
- Beginner

How much I loved this project ♡
◇ ◇ ◇ ◇ ◇

stick picture here

Name of design:

Canvas size: _____
Picture size: _____
Square drill ☐   Round drill ○

I purchased this kit from: _____
(or it was gifted by)

Price: ☐

- Advanced
- Intermediate
- Beginner

Date started: / / /
Date of completion: / / /

How much I loved this project ♡
◇ ◇ ◇ ◇ ◇

After the completion of this piece I:
Kept it for myself ◇   Sold it ◇
Gifted it to a loved one ◇   Other ◇

I gifted it to: _____
Or I sold it for ☐ on/at _____
_____ on the / / /

Notes & ideas for the next project:
_____
_____
_____
_____

stick picture here

Name of design:

Canvas size: _____
Picture size: _____
Square drill ☐   Round drill ○

I purchased this kit from:
(or it was gifted by)
_____
Price: ☐

After the completion of this piece I:
Kept it for myself ◇   Sold it ◇
Gifted it to a loved one ◇   Other ◇

I gifted it to: _____
Or I sold it for ☐ on/at _____
_____ on the / / /

Notes & ideas for the next project:
_____
_____
_____
_____

Date started: / / /
Date of completion: / / /

Advanced
Intermediate
Beginner

How much I loved this project ♡
◇ ◇ ◇ ◇ ◇

stick picture here

Name of design:

Canvas size: _____
Picture size: _____
Square drill ☐   Round drill ○

Date started: _/_/_
Date of completion: _/_/_

I purchased this kit from:
(or it was gifted by)

- Advanced
- Intermediate
- Beginner

How much I loved this project ♡
◇ ◇ ◇ ◇ ◇

_____

Price: ☐

After the completion of this piece I:

Kept it for myself ◇   Sold it ◇
Gifted it to a loved one ◇   Other ◇

I gifted it to: _____
Or I sold it for ☐ on/at _____
_____ on the _/_/_

Notes & ideas for the next project:
_____
_____
_____
_____

stick picture here

Name of design:

Canvas size: _____
Picture size: _____
Square drill ☐   Round drill ○

I purchased this kit from:
(or it was gifted by)
_____

Price: [_____]

Advanced
Intermediate
Beginner

Date started: / / /
Date of completion: / / /

How much I loved this project ♡
◇ ◇ ◇ ◇ ◇

After the completion of this piece I:

Kept it for myself ◇   Sold it ◇
Gifted it to a loved one ◇   Other ◇

I gifted it to: _____
Or I sold it for [_____] on/at _____
_____ on the / / /

Notes & ideas for the next project:
_____
_____
_____
_____

stick picture here

Name of design:

Canvas size: _____
Picture size: _____
Square drill ☐   Round drill ○

I purchased this kit from:
(or it was gifted by)
_____
Price: ☐

Date started: / /
Date of completion: / /

- Advanced
- Intermediate
- Beginner

How much I loved this project ♡
◇ ◇ ◇ ◇ ◇

After the completion of this piece I:
Kept it for myself ◇   Sold it ◇
Gifted it to a loved one ◇   Other ◇

I gifted it to: _____
Or I sold it for ☐ on/at _____
_____ on the / /

Notes & ideas for the next project:
_____
_____
_____
_____

stick picture here

Name of Design:

Canvas size: _____
Picture size: _____
Square drill ☐   Round drill ○

I purchased this kit from:
(or it was gifted by)
_____
Price: ☐

After the completion of this piece I:
Kept it for myself ◇   Sold it ◇
Gifted it to a loved one ◇   Other ◇

I gifted it to: _____
Or I sold it for ☐ on/at _____
_____ on the / / /

Notes & ideas for the next project:
_____
_____
_____
_____

Date started: / / /
Date of completion: / / /

Advanced
Intermediate
Beginner

How much I loved this project ♥
◇ ◇ ◇ ◇ ◇

stick picture here

Name of design:

Canvas size: _____
Picture size: _____
Square drill ☐   Round drill ○

I purchased this kit from:
(or it was gifted by)

_____
Price: ☐

Advanced
Intermediate
Beginner

Date started: / /
Date of completion: / /

How much I loved this project ♡
◇ ◇ ◇ ◇ ◇

After the completion of this piece I:
Kept it for myself ◇   Sold it ◇
Gifted it to a loved one ◇   Other ◇

I gifted it to: _____
Or I sold it for ☐ on/at _____
_____ on the / /

Notes & ideas for the next project:
_____
_____
_____
_____

stick picture here

Name of design:

Canvas size: _____
Picture size: _____
Square drill ☐   Round drill ○

I purchased this kit from:
(or it was gifted by)
_____

Price: [ ]

Advanced
Intermediate
Beginner

Date started: / /
Date of completion: / /

How much I loved this project ♡
◇ ◇ ◇ ◇ ◇

After the completion of this piece I:
Kept it for myself ◇   Sold it ◇
Gifted it to a loved one ◇   Other ◇

I gifted it to: _____
Or I sold it for [ ] on/at _____
_____ on the / /

Notes & ideas for the next project:
_____
_____
_____
_____

stick picture here

Name of design:

Canvas size: _____
Picture size: _____
Square drill ☐   Round drill ○

I purchased this kit from:
(or it was gifted by)
_____

Price: [   ]

Date started: _ / _ / _
Date of completion: _ / _ / _

- Advanced
- Intermediate
- Beginner

How much I loved this project ♡
◇ ◇ ◇ ◇ ◇

After the completion of this piece I:
Kept it for myself ◇   Sold it ◇
Gifted it to a loved one ◇   Other ◇

I gifted it to: _____
Or I sold it for [   ] on/at _____
_____ on the _ / _ / _

Notes & ideas for the next project:
_____
_____
_____
_____

stick picture here

◇·◇·◇·◇·◇·◇·◇·◇·◇·◇·◇·◇·◇·◇

Name of design:

Canvas size: _____
Picture size: _____
Square drill ☐   Round drill ○

I purchased this kit from:
(or it was gifted by)
_____
Price: [____]

After the completion of this piece I:
Kept it for myself ◇   Sold it ◇
Gifted it to a loved one ◇   Other ◇

I gifted it to: _____
Or I sold it for [____] on/at _____
_____ on the / / /

Notes & ideas for the next project:
_____
_____
_____
_____

Date started: / / /
Date of completion: / / /

Advanced
Intermediate
Beginner

How much I loved this project ♡
◇ ◇ ◇ ◇ ◇

stick picture here

Name of design:

Canvas size: _____
Picture size: _____
Square drill ☐   Round drill ○

I purchased this kit from:
(or it was gifted by)
_____
Price: [____]

Advanced
Intermediate
Beginner

Date started: / / /
Date of completion: / / /

How much I loved this project ♡
◇ ◇ ◇ ◇ ◇

After the completion of this piece I:
Kept it for myself ◇   Sold it ◇
Gifted it to a loved one ◇   Other ◇

I gifted it to: _____
Or I sold it for [____] on/at _____
_____ on the / / /

Notes & ideas for the next project:
_____
_____
_____
_____

stick picture here

NAME OF DESIGN:

CANVAS SIZE: _____
PICTURE SIZE: _____
SQUARE DRILL ☐   ROUND DRILL ○

I PURCHASED THIS KIT FROM:
(OR IT WAS GIFTED BY)
_____

PRICE: ☐

DATE STARTED: / / /
DATE OF COMPLETION: / / /

ADVANCED
INTERMEDIATE
BEGINNER

HOW MUCH I LOVED THIS PROJECT ♡
◇ ◇ ◇ ◇ ◇

AFTER THE COMPLETION OF THIS PIECE I:
KEPT IT FOR MYSELF ◇   SOLD IT ◇
GIFTED IT TO A LOVED ONE ◇   OTHER ◇

I GIFTED IT TO: _____
OR I SOLD IT FOR ☐ ON/AT _____
_____ ON THE / / /

NOTES & IDEAS FOR THE NEXT PROJECT:
_____
_____
_____
_____

stick picture here

NAME OF DESIGN:

CANVAS SIZE: _____
PICTURE SIZE: _____
SQUARE DRILL ☐   ROUND DRILL ○

DATE STARTED: / / /
DATE OF COMPLETION: / / /

I PURCHASED THIS KIT FROM:
(OR IT WAS GIFTED BY)
_____
PRICE: [ ]

- ADVANCED
- INTERMEDIATE
- BEGINNER

HOW MUCH I LOVED THIS PROJECT ♡
◇ ◇ ◇ ◇ ◇

AFTER THE COMPLETION OF THIS PIECE I:
KEPT IT FOR MYSELF ◇   SOLD IT ◇
GIFTED IT TO A LOVED ONE ◇   OTHER ◇

I GIFTED IT TO: _____
OR I SOLD IT FOR [ ]   ON/AT _____
_____ ON THE / / /

NOTES & IDEAS FOR THE NEXT PROJECT:
_____
_____
_____
_____

stick picture here

NAME OF DESIGN:

CANVAS SIZE: _____
PICTURE SIZE: _____
SQUARE DRILL ☐   ROUND DRILL ◯

I PURCHASED THIS KIT FROM:
(OR IT WAS GIFTED BY)
_____
PRICE: ☐

DATE STARTED: / /
DATE OF COMPLETION: / /

ADVANCED
INTERMEDIATE
BEGINNER

HOW MUCH I LOVED THIS PROJECT ♡
◇ ◇ ◇ ◇ ◇

AFTER THE COMPLETION OF THIS PIECE I:
KEPT IT FOR MYSELF ◇   SOLD IT ◇
GIFTED IT TO A LOVED ONE ◇   OTHER ◇
I GIFTED IT TO: _____
OR I SOLD IT FOR ☐ ON/AT _____
_____ ON THE / /

NOTES & IDEAS FOR THE NEXT PROJECT:
_____
_____
_____
_____

stick picture here

Name of design:

Canvas size: _____
Picture size: _____
Square drill ☐ Round drill ○

I purchased this kit from:
(or it was gifted by)
_____

Price: ☐

Advanced
Intermediate
Beginner

Date started: / / /
Date of completion: / / /

How much I loved this project ♡
◇ ◇ ◇ ◇ ◇

After the completion of this piece I:
Kept it for myself ◇ Sold it ◇
Gifted it to a loved one ◇ Other ◇

I gifted it to: _____
Or I sold it for ☐ on/at _____
_____ on the / / /

Notes & ideas for the next project:
_____
_____
_____
_____

stick picture here

Name of design:

Canvas size: _____

Picture size: _____

Square drill ☐   Round drill ○

I purchased this kit from:
(or it was gifted by)
_____

Price: [ ]

Date started: / / /

Date of completion: / / /

Advanced
Intermediate
Beginner

How much I loved this project ♡
◇ ◇ ◇ ◇ ◇

After the completion of this piece I:

Kept it for myself ◇   Sold it ◇

Gifted it to a loved one ◇   Other ◇

I gifted it to: _____

Or I sold it for [ ]   On/at _____

_____ On the / / /

Notes & ideas for the next project:

_____
_____
_____
_____

◇·◇·◇·◇·◇·◇·◇·◇·◇·◇·◇·◇·◇·◇·◇·◇·◇

stick picture here

NAME OF DESIGN:

CANVAS SIZE: _____
PICTURE SIZE: _____
SQUARE DRILL ☐   ROUND DRILL ◯

I PURCHASED THIS KIT FROM:
(OR IT WAS GIFTED BY)
_____
PRICE: [ ]

DATE STARTED: / / /
DATE OF COMPLETION: / / /

ADVANCED
INTERMEDIATE
BEGINNER

HOW MUCH I LOVED THIS PROJECT ♡
◇ ◇ ◇ ◇ ◇

AFTER THE COMPLETION OF THIS PIECE I:
KEPT IT FOR MYSELF ◇   SOLD IT ◇
GIFTED IT TO A LOVED ONE ◇   OTHER ◇

I GIFTED IT TO: _____
OR I SOLD IT FOR [ ] ON/AT _____
_____ ON THE / / /

NOTES & IDEAS FOR THE NEXT PROJECT:
_____
_____
_____
_____

stick picture here

Name of design:

Canvas size: _____
Picture size: _____
Square drill ☐   Round drill ○

I purchased this kit from: _____
(or it was gifted by)

Price: [ ]

After the completion of this piece I:
Kept it for myself ◇   Sold it ◇
Gifted it to a loved one ◇   Other ◇

I gifted it to: _____
Or I sold it for [ ]   on/at _____
_____   on the / /

Notes & ideas for the next project:
_____
_____
_____
_____

Date started: / /
Date of completion: / /

Advanced
Intermediate
Beginner

How much I loved this project ♡
◇ ◇ ◇ ◇ ◇

stick picture here

NAME OF DESIGN:

CANVAS SIZE: _____
PICTURE SIZE: _____
SQUARE DRILL ☐   ROUND DRILL ○

DATE STARTED: / / /
DATE OF COMPLETION: / / /

I PURCHASED THIS KIT FROM:
(OR IT WAS GIFTED BY)
_____

ADVANCED
INTERMEDIATE
BEGINNER

HOW MUCH I LOVED THIS PROJECT ♡
◇ ◇ ◇ ◇ ◇

PRICE: ☐

AFTER THE COMPLETION OF THIS PIECE I:
KEPT IT FOR MYSELF ◇   SOLD IT ◇
GIFTED IT TO A LOVED ONE ◇   OTHER ◇

I GIFTED IT TO: _____
OR I SOLD IT FOR ☐ ON/AT _____
_____ ON THE / / /

NOTES & IDEAS FOR THE NEXT PROJECT:
_____
_____
_____
_____

◇·◇·◇·◇·◇·◇·◇·◇·◇·◇·◇·◇·◇·◇

stick picture here

Name of design:

Canvas size: _____
Picture size: _____
Square drill ☐   Round drill ○

I purchased this kit from:
(or it was gifted by)
_____

Price: ☐

After the completion of this piece I:
Kept it for myself ◇   Sold it ◇
Gifted it to a loved one ◇   Other ◇

I gifted it to: _____
Or I sold it for ☐ on/at _____
_____ on the / / /

Notes & ideas for the next project:
_____
_____
_____
_____

Date started: / / /
Date of completion: / / /

Advanced
Intermediate
Beginner

How much I loved this project ♡
◇ ◇ ◇ ◇ ◇

stick picture here

Name of design:

Canvas size: _____
Picture size: _____
Square drill ☐ Round drill ○

I purchased this kit from:
(or it was gifted by)
_____

Price: ☐

Advanced
Intermediate
Beginner

Date started: / / /
Date of completion: / / /

How much I loved this project ♡
◇ ◇ ◇ ◇ ◇

After the completion of this piece I:
Kept it for myself ◇   Sold it ◇
Gifted it to a loved one ◇   Other ◇

I gifted it to: _____
Or I sold it for ☐ on/at _____
_____ on the / / /

Notes & ideas for the next project:
_____
_____
_____
_____

stick picture here

Name of design:

Canvas size: _____
Picture size: _____
Square drill ☐   Round drill ○

I purchased this kit from:
(or it was gifted by)
_____

Price: [ ]

After the completion of this piece I:
Kept it for myself ◇   Sold it ◇
Gifted it to a loved one ◇   Other ◇

I gifted it to: _____
Or I sold it for [ ] on/at _____
_____ on the / / /

Notes & ideas for the next project:
_____
_____
_____
_____

Date started: / / /
Date of completion: / / /

Advanced
Intermediate
Beginner

How much I loved this project ♡
◇ ◇ ◇ ◇ ◇

stick picture here

Name of design:

Canvas size: _____
Picture size: _____
Square drill ☐   Round drill ○

I purchased this kit from:
(or it was gifted by)
_____

Price: [____]

Advanced
Intermediate
Beginner

Date started: _/_/_
Date of completion: _/_/_

How much I loved this project ♡
◇ ◇ ◇ ◇ ◇

After the completion of this piece I:
Kept it for myself ◇   Sold it ◇
Gifted it to a loved one ◇   Other ◇

I gifted it to: _____
Or I sold it for [____] on/at _____
_____ on the _/_/_

Notes & ideas for the next project:
_____
_____
_____
_____

stick picture here

Name of design:

Canvas size: _____
Picture size: _____
Square drill ☐   Round drill ○

I purchased this kit from:
(or it was gifted by)

_____

Price: [ ]

Advanced
Intermediate
Beginner

Date started: / /
Date of completion: / /

How much I loved this project ♡
◇ ◇ ◇ ◇ ◇

After the completion of this piece I:

Kept it for myself ◇   Sold it ◇
Gifted it to a loved one ◇   Other ◇

I gifted it to: _____
Or I sold it for [ ] on/at _____
_____ on the / /

Notes & ideas for the next project:

_____
_____
_____
_____

stick picture here

Name of design:

Canvas size: _____
Picture size: _____
Square drill ☐   Round drill ○

Date started: _/_/_
Date of completion: _/_/_

I purchased this kit from: _____
(or it was gifted by)

Advanced
Intermediate
Beginner

How much I loved this project ♡
◇ ◇ ◇ ◇ ◇

Price: [____]

After the completion of this piece I:
Kept it for myself ◇   Sold it ◇
Gifted it to a loved one ◇   Other ◇

I gifted it to: _____
Or I sold it for [____] on/at _____
_____ on the _/_/_

Notes & ideas for the next project:
_____
_____
_____
_____

◇◇◇◇◇◇◇◇◇◇◇◇◇◇◇◇

stick picture here

Name of Design:

Canvas size: _____
Picture size: _____
Square drill ☐   Round drill ○

I purchased this kit from:
(or it was gifted by)
_____

Price: ☐

- Advanced
- Intermediate
- Beginner

Date started: / / /
Date of completion: / / /

How much I loved this project ♡
◇ ◇ ◇ ◇ ◇

After the completion of this piece I:
Kept it for myself ◇   Sold it ◇
Gifted it to a loved one ◇   Other ◇

I gifted it to:_____
Or I sold it for ☐ on/at _____
_____ on the / / /

Notes & ideas for the next project:
_____
_____
_____
_____

stick picture here

Name of design:

Canvas size: _____
Picture size: _____
Square drill ☐   Round drill ○

I purchased this kit from: _____
(or it was gifted by) _____

Price: ☐

- Advanced
- Intermediate
- Beginner

Date started: _ / _ / _
Date of completion: _ / _ / _

How much I loved this project ♡
◇ ◇ ◇ ◇ ◇

After the completion of this piece I:
Kept it for myself ◇   Sold it ◇
Gifted it to a loved one ◇   Other ◇

I gifted it to: _____
Or I sold it for ☐ on/at _____
_____ on the _ / _ / _

Notes & ideas for the next project:
_____
_____
_____
_____

stick picture here

Name of design:

Canvas size: _____
Picture size: _____
Square drill ☐   Round drill ○

I purchased this kit from:
(or it was gifted by)
_____
Price: [____]

Date started: _/_/_
Date of completion: _/_/_

Advanced
Intermediate
Beginner

How much I loved this project ♡
◇ ◇ ◇ ◇ ◇

After the completion of this piece I:

Kept it for myself ◇   Sold it ◇

Gifted it to a loved one ◇   Other ◇

I gifted it to:_____
Or I sold it for [____] on/at_____
_____ on the _/_/_

Notes & ideas for the next project:
_____
_____
_____
_____

stick picture here

◇◇◇◇◇◇◇◇◇◇◇◇◇◇◇◇◇

Name of Design:

Canvas size: _____
Picture size: _____
Square drill ☐   Round drill ○

Date started: _ / _ / _
Date of completion: _ / _ / _

I purchased this kit from:
(or it was gifted by)
_____

Price: [ ]

- Advanced
- Intermediate
- Beginner

How much I loved this project ♡
◇ ◇ ◇ ◇ ◇

After the completion of this piece I:
Kept it for myself ◇   Sold it ◇
Gifted it to a loved one ◇   Other ◇

I gifted it to: _____
Or I sold it for [ ] on/at _____
_____ on the _ / _ / _

Notes & ideas for the next project:
_____
_____
_____
_____

stick picture here

Name of Design:

Canvas size: _____
Picture size: _____
Square drill ☐   Round drill ○

I purchased this kit from:
(or it was gifted by)
_____
Price: [____]

Date started: / /
Date of completion: / /

Advanced / Intermediate / Beginner

How much I loved this project ♡
◇ ◇ ◇ ◇ ◇

After the completion of this piece I:
Kept it for myself ◇   Sold it ◇
Gifted it to a loved one ◇   Other ◇

I gifted it to: _____
Or I sold it for [____] on/at _____
_____ on the / /

Notes & ideas for the next project:
_____
_____
_____
_____

stick picture here

Name of design:

Canvas size: _____

Picture size: _____

Square drill ☐   Round drill ○

Date started: _/_/_

Date of completion: _/_/_

I purchased this kit from:
(or it was gifted by)

- Advanced
- Intermediate
- Beginner

How much I loved this project ♡
◇ ◇ ◇ ◇ ◇

_____

Price: ☐

After the completion of this piece I:

Kept it for myself ◇   Sold it ◇

Gifted it to a loved one ◇   Other ◇

I gifted it to: _____

Or I sold it for ☐ on/at _____

_____ on the _/_/_

Notes & ideas for the next project:

_____
_____
_____
_____

stick picture here

Name of design:

Canvas size: _____
Picture size: _____
Square drill ☐   Round drill ○

I purchased this kit from:
(or it was gifted by)
_____
Price: [ ]

Advanced
Intermediate
Beginner

Date started: _/_/_
Date of completion: _/_/_

How much I loved this project ♡
◇ ◇ ◇ ◇ ◇

After the completion of this piece I:
Kept it for myself ◇   Sold it ◇
Gifted it to a loved one ◇   Other ◇

I gifted it to: _____
Or I sold it for [ ] on/at _____
_____ on the _/_/_

Notes & ideas for the next project:
_____
_____
_____
_____

stick picture here

Name of design:

Canvas size: _____
Picture size: _____
Square drill ☐   Round drill ○

I purchased this kit from:
(or it was gifted by)
_____

Price: [　　　]

After the completion of this piece I:
Kept it for myself ◇   Sold it ◇
Gifted it to a loved one ◇   Other ◇

I gifted it to: _____
Or I sold it for [　　　] on/at _____
_____ on the / / /

Notes & ideas for the next project:
_____
_____
_____
_____

Date started: / / /
Date of completion: / / /

Advanced
Intermediate
Beginner

How much I loved this project ♡
◇ ◇ ◇ ◇ ◇

stick picture here

Name of design:

Canvas size: _____
Picture size: _____
Square drill ☐   Round drill ○

I purchased this kit from: _____
(or it was gifted by)
_____

Price: ☐

Date started: / /
Date of completion: / /

Advanced
Intermediate
Beginner

How much I loved this project ♡
◇ ◇ ◇ ◇ ◇

After the completion of this piece I:
Kept it for myself ◇   Sold it ◇
Gifted it to a loved one ◇   Other ◇
I gifted it to: _____
Or I sold it for ☐ on/at _____
_____ on the / /

Notes & ideas for the next project:
_____
_____
_____
_____

stick picture here

Name of design:

Canvas size: _____
Picture size: _____
Square drill ☐   Round drill ○

I purchased this kit from:
(or it was gifted by)
_____
Price: ☐

Advanced
Intermediate
Beginner

Date started: / / /
Date of completion: / / /

How much I loved this project ♡
◇ ◇ ◇ ◇ ◇

After the completion of this piece I:
Kept it for myself ◇   Sold it ◇
Gifted it to a loved one ◇   Other ◇
I gifted it to: _____
Or I sold it for ☐ on/at _____
_____ on the / / /

Notes & ideas for the next project:
_____
_____
_____
_____

stick picture here

Name of design:

Canvas size: _____
Picture size: _____
Square drill ☐   Round drill ◯

I purchased this kit from: _____
(or it was gifted by)

Price: ☐

- Advanced
- Intermediate
- Beginner

Date started: / /
Date of completion: / /

How much I loved this project ♡
◇ ◇ ◇ ◇ ◇

After the completion of this piece I:
Kept it for myself ◇   Sold it ◇
Gifted it to a loved one ◇   Other ◇

I gifted it to: _____
Or I sold it for ☐ on/at _____
_____ on the / /

Notes & ideas for the next project:
_____
_____
_____
_____

◇◦◇◦◇◦◇◦◇◦◇◦◇◦◇◦◇◦◇◦◇

stick picture here

Name of Design:

Canvas size: _____
Picture size: _____
Square drill ☐   Round drill ○

Date started: _ / _ / _
Date of completion: _ / _ / _

I purchased this kit from:
(or it was gifted by)

◇ Advanced
◇ Intermediate
◇ Beginner

How much I loved this project ♡
◇ ◇ ◇ ◇ ◇

_____
Price: ☐

After the completion of this piece I:
Kept it for myself ◇   Sold it ◇
Gifted it to a loved one ◇   Other ◇

I gifted it to: _____
Or I sold it for ☐ on/at _____
_____ on the _ / _ / _

Notes & ideas for the next project:
_____
_____
_____
_____

stick picture here

Name of design:

Canvas size: _____
Picture size: _____
Square drill ☐   Round drill ○

I purchased this kit from:
(or it was gifted by)
_____

Price: [ ]

Advanced
Intermediate
Beginner

Date started: / /
Date of completion: / /

How much I loved this project ♡
◇ ◇ ◇ ◇ ◇

After the completion of this piece I:
Kept it for myself ◇   Sold it ◇
Gifted it to a loved one ◇   Other ◇

I gifted it to: _____
Or I sold it for [ ] on/at _____
_____ on the / /

Notes & ideas for the next project:
_____
_____
_____
_____

stick picture here

Name of design: _____

Canvas size: _____
Picture size: _____
Square drill ☐   Round drill ○

I purchased this kit from:
(or it was gifted by)
_____
Price: [ ]

Date started: / / /
Date of completion: / / /

- Advanced
- Intermediate
- Beginner

How much I loved this project ♡
◇ ◇ ◇ ◇ ◇

After the completion of this piece I:
Kept it for myself ◇   Sold it ◇
Gifted it to a loved one ◇   Other ◇

I gifted it to: _____
Or I sold it for [ ] on/at _____
_____ on the / / /

Notes & ideas for the next project:
_____
_____
_____
_____

stick picture here

◇◇◇◇◇◇◇◇◇◇◇◇◇◇◇◇◇◇

Made in the USA
Las Vegas, NV
19 February 2024